Diary of a Sent-Down Youth

Diary of a Sent-Down Youth

Luo Ying

Translated by Denis Mair

WHITE PINE PRESS / BUFFALO, NEW YORK

White Pine Press
P.O. Box 236
Buffalo, NY 14201
www.whitepine.org

Cover image: ⓐ April 30,1964. Source: 《人民画报》1964年第4期
            Author: 人民画报

Book Design: Elaine LaMattina

Printed and bound in the United States of America.

ISBN: 978-1-945680-77-9

Library of Congress number 2024930189

Diary of a Sent-Down Youth

Contents

Introduction

Prior to Mao Zedong's establishment of the People's Republic of China on October 1, 1949, China had been a largely agrarian society. Mao believed that to become a player on the world stage, China needed to industrialize, and the Soviet Union was ready and willing to help. When Mao announced that the communist bloc would be its principal ally, it seemed to be a new beginning for a country that had suffered through a two-decade long civil war between Chiang Kai-shek's Nationalists and the Mao's Communists .

By 1956, when Huang Yuping—who would later take the pen name Luo Ying—was born in the western Chinese city of Lanzhou, cracks in the Sino-Soviet alliance had begun to appear, due, in part, to Mao's fears that the Soviet Union would ultimately try to take control of China.

"Listen carefully," said Mao. "We have worked long and hard to drive out the Americans, the British, the Japanese, and others. Never again will we allow foreigners to use our territory for their purposes."

In 1958, Huang Yuping's family moved to Yinchuan, a city in Ningxia Province in the north of China. That same year, Mao broke with the Soviet Union and announced a new economic program, the "Great Leap Forward," intended to raise industrial and agricultural production. Within a year, almost all Chinese villages were working communes where several thousand people lived and worked together.

But Mao's concerns extended beyond the Soviets. He had begun to believe that some of his military commanders had questionable loyalty to him, and he embarked on a series of purges. Huang Yuping's father, Huang Junfu, who had served honorably as a colonel in the Northwest Guerilla Corps, came to be seen as a counter-revolutionary during one of those purges and was sent to the Xihu Prison Farm.

In 1959, after suffering abuse and terrible living conditions in the prison, he became very ill. Consequently, he saved up his medications for three months and then swallowed a fatal dose. He was buried in an unmarked grave in the desert.

> When they buried him in the dunes,
> his eyes were still staring,
>
> An enemy got no gravestone,
> so he rotted like a nameless dog.

His wife, Yan Xiuying, was left with four small children to raise on her own. Huang Yuping was just three years old. He and his family were now known as the family of a counter-revolutionary, and their lives were made miserable.

He died like a dog, and I had to live like one.

His mother was reduced to selling dirt to support her children:

> Each day she dug up dirt and sold it
> ...she pulled her wooden cart out the gate
> A woman in her thirties, harnessed like a mule
> When she passed, kids on the street
> mimicked her wails and stomping
> When she passed, neighbors along the street
> pursed their lips in contempt
> Shamelessly she scavenged
> cabbage leaves and bone scraps

From 1960 to 1961, a combination of the government's poor planning, unusual weather patterns, and natural disasters resulted in widespread famine and a likely death toll of between twenty and forty million. When Mao finally accepted the fact that the Great Leap Forward had failed, he relinquished power. The task of turning things around fell to others, and they managed to engineer an almost miraculous recovery.

In 1966, however, Mao sought, successfully, to return to absolute power again. He launched the Great Proletarian Cultural Revolution, claiming that bourgeois elements had infiltrated the government and society with the aim of restoring capitalism. Mao called on young people to resist this and proclaimed that "to rebel is justified." Many young people, mainly students, responded by forming cadres of Red Guards throughout the country. Despite the years of being stigmatized and tormented by the villagers as the son of a counter-revolutionary, Huang became an enthusiastic Red Guard. One of his poems describes him punching a landowner—who later died—with his "steel fists."[1]

A variety of factors, including urban unemployment and the Cultural Revolution's disruption of the education system, led Mao to proclaim in 1968 that it was necessary for educated urban youth to be sent to the countryside and undergo reeducation by the poor peasants. The program was meant to both cultivate the sent-down youth's commitment to party ideology and to foster economic growth in underdeveloped areas.

Huang's mother died suddenly in 1969, and at the age of thirteen he was left to fend for himself, scavaging for food to keep himself and his siblings alive. Three years later, as he was watching the waves of the Yellow River crash into its banks one day, he decided to change his name from Yuping, (Jade Peace) to Nubo, (Angry Wave) in an attempt to change his life.

"I made a resolution to join a production brigade and bid farewell to my former life. I wasn't calm, I was angry."[2]

Joining the ranks of some twenty million sent-down youth, he was sent to Tonggui county near Yinchuan, where he worked alongside farmers. He formed a basketball team, joined the Communist Party, and, in 1976, began writing poetry.

The death of Mao in September of 1976 paved the way for change. University entrance exams restarted in 1977, and Ningxia Province was given a single place at Peking University to award to a local student. Huang Nubo was put forward as he was considered "educated, able to write poetry, and supported by the masses."[3]

Also in 1977, Deng Xiaoping, a revolutionary and statesman in Mao's government, began a rise to power, culminating in him becoming China's paramount leader in December 1978. Deng and his allies then began to open the door for a transition to a more market-oriented economic system, initiating a program that introduced elements of market capitalism to the Chinese economy. In August 1980, Deng and his allies embarked on a series of political reforms. These reforms gradually led China away from a command economy and Maoist dogma, opened it up to foreign investments and technology, and introduced its vast labor force to the global market thereby transforming China into one of the world's fastest-growing economies.[4]

After graduating from Peking University in 1981, Huang found a job in the Central Propaganda Department of the Communist Party. He rose to become a department director. His official career was looking bright, but he had started to feel uneasy. A turning point seems to have come at the age of twenty-nine, when he read Anton Chekhov's short story, "The Death of a Government Clerk," which, he says, "brought out a cold sweat."[5]

He left his government position and went into business, starting off doing small deals buying and selling goods. Encouraged by his success, in 1995 he set up his own company, Zhongkun Investment Group. He began with real estate, and after having tremendous success, branched out into tourism. Today, his conglomerate plays an important role in preserving Chinese cultural treasures, such as the architecturally-intact Ming Dynasty village Hongcun in Anhui Provincen, as well as running tours to cultural and archeological sites, including the 4000-year-old Xiaohe Cemetery, remnant of a once-flourishing Central Asian kingdom along the old Silk Road.

A self-made billionaire, Huang is also an intrepid mountaineer who has summited the highest peaks on every continent, and, under the pen name Luo Ying, a successful poet whose work has been translated and published internationally.

Although the Communist Party had, in 1981, officially pronounced the Cultural Revolution a grave error that "led to domestic turmoil and brought catastrophe to the Party, the state, and the whole people,"[6] Huang believes that the Cultural Revolution and sent-down experience made him and his generation what they are. They were given, he has said, wills of steel, learned how to live with hardship, and how to relentlessly pursue their goals.

"The Cultural Revolution taught this generation of mine that you must act like a wolf in order to survive," he explained.

It destroyed old value systems and replaced them with the belief "that winner takes all, that if you can beat someone, then you're a hero, that if you're rich, you're in the right."[7]

"All we pursue is profit and money. But when you really get your hands on it, you feel anguished and disappointed, and you don't know if any of it means anything."[8]

Many of the Sent-Down Youth have gone on to become important business people and leaders in China, including Chinese President Xi Jinping, internationally acclaimed filmmaker Zhang Yimou, and Ren Jianxin, founder of China National Chemical Corporation. Yet Huang dreads a repetition of his past.

As many of the era's horrors are slowly forgotten, nostalgia for some aspects persists in certain quarters: television shows romanticize the lives of sent-down youths, and there are more than fifty museums about them around the country. Huang decries this whitewashing of history.

"If we continue on like this and don't reflect on this past, there will be another Cultural Revolution," he has said. "If the impression left behind is that the Cultural Revolution was so romantic, people won't be afraid to turn once again to brutality."[9]

He feels a responsibility to record what he witnessed. He has written about these years in a previous book, *Memories of the Cultural Revolution*, published by the University of Oklahoma Press in 2015. The book had been banned in China due to the chilling images it presents of the horrors of that era.

This book is the first he wrote about his experiences and is less directly critical. Many of the poems are portraits of other sent-down youth, some of whom he reunited with in later years. A common thread with many of them is that they refuse to acknowledge their experiences.

"When at the end you look at your current position in society, you'll think back and wonder whether the nightmare you lived through was in fact right or not," Huang has said. "But the harm it's brought to your heart can never be got rid of in a lifetime."[10]

—Elaine LaMattina

Excerpts from poems on page 12 are from *Memories of the Cultural Revolution*, translated by Denis Mair and published by the University of Oklahoma Press in 2015.

1. *Straits Times*, "Cultural Revolution Demons Haunt Chinese Billionaire Huang Nubo." May 16, 2016
2. Ibid.
3. Zhang Yuquan. *Dialogue Earth*. "China's Icelandic Conquerer." October 26, 2011.
4. "China's Post-1978 Economic Development and Entry into the Global Trading System." The Cato Institute. Washington, D.C., October 10, 2023.
5. Zhang Yuquan. *Dialogue Earth*.
6. *Straits Times*
7. Ibid.
8. Ned Levin. "Chinese Tycoons Lay Bare Existential Angst, Obedient Sheep." London: *Financial Times*. November 26, 2013.
9. *Straits Times*.
10. Zhang Yuquan.

Diary of a Sent-Down Youth

A Youth Named Yi Zhongren

Back then he was an educated youth
reassigned to his own home district
He danced, played fiddle, headed our Youth League branch
On midwinter days when the sun broke through
he'd sit on one end of my heated-brick bed
smoking and sipping liquor
Peeping through a hole in the newspaper
he'd report on the physical endowments of sent-down girls
Once, riding his bike to the city, a girl sitting behind him,
he fell over into a roadside field and wound up with a black eye
Afterward, he brayed like an excited donkey
claiming he'd touched her breast while rolling in the wheat
He adamantly insisted that he'd copped a feel
but most likely he didn't succeed

During militia training
he lost an index finger
when he touched the fuse of an anti-tank mine
I thought he was just absentminded

But not much later, he lost a little finger
after having an affair with his brother's wife
His brother's reproaches triggered a family argument
so he picked up a butcher knife and cut his own finger off
A rooster rushed in, snatched the finger in its beak,
then dashed away to where no-one could find it
It was truly a human tragedy
that such a miserable thing happened
You see, she'd been his childhood sweetheart
but the marriage had been arranged by his father

One winter night we stayed up drinking a one-catty bottle
of sweet potato wine that cost 1.18 yuan

That night I forgot
to snuff the brazier and open a vent
The next day, I thought I'd die
My friend, although vomiting, crawled to the door
and cried out
Who will ever marry me?
Will anyone ever marry me?

In 2006, during the rainy season in our province
I went back to that town and met him for a drink
He wore a hat all evening to hide his baldness
When I brought up past events, he said they never happened

I chuckled and raised my glass, but my heart felt a pang
That's right, those things could *never* have happened

Miss Wu Yafang

You probably know that our commune's cultural troupe
had an abundance of beauties, like a flock of butterflies
This, of course, was the judgment young bachelors made
during late-night conversations under the glow of an oil lamp
Wu Yafang was the liveliest spark in that troupe
Short in stature with big round eyes and crimson lips,
when she danced it was like watching a skylark in flight
All the sent-down guys were entranced by her
It was, of course, my constant wish
to sit close to her and hear her voice

But she loved one of the older guys
although he had his sights set on other girls

One day, riding our bikes back to town
we heard water gurgling in a willow-shaded stream
The sky resounded with the chirr of cicadas
I felt droplets of their excrement
hitting my head and clothes like little pinpricks
I wanted to talk with her about Shelley and Pushkin
She quoted lines from Mayakovsky and Yesenin
I praised the kind of steadfast love shown in *The Gadfly*
She found beauty in Lin Daojing's revolutionary love
Of course, the older student she liked had read *Das Kapital*

I still remember that as a day
of pure romance

I still remember that as the day
we basked in the human warmth of. our town

You probably already know
how infatuation passes quickly by
She was like a swallow, flitting before our eyes

But one day her eyes looked puffy from crying
Her older crush had been called to work in the city
That seemed to be too big a blow for her
She no longer danced or spent time with young men
When I left, she wouldn't shake my hand
She wouldn't even bid me a revolutionary farewell

Much later, after perhaps twenty years,
she passed through Beijing on a trip with her daughter
I went to her small hotel, and we talked about the past
She sat before me in a prim and proper pose
saying we'd better not give her daughter the wrong idea

That's right, we wouldn't want children to get the wrong idea

Rainbow Jin

Rainbow Jin, an only child, was my basketball buddy
I played guard and he played forward
He was more accurate than I at shooting hoops
His appeal to the girls was greater than mine, too
A bit jealous, I said he moved too slowly on the court
Girls compared us, said his movements were graceful and effortless
While we planted rice sprouts, girls clustered around him
One dayI planted five rows of sprouts while he planted seven
The girls gladly brought plants and filled in his gaps

One evening the following autumn, during the harvest
our commune was showing movies in the courtyard
He lay alone on a bed complaining of a stomach ache
As it turned out, he died that very night
of a heart attack brought on by methane poisoning
He was buried on a ridge in the Helan Mountains
Later my mother was buried there, not far from him

Eventually, his grave was covered with withered grass
and no one brought offerings on Tomb Sweeping Day
but I used red paint to retrace the words on his plaque:

> Grave of the student Rainbow Jin,
> who was sent to the countryside
>
> Died September 14, 1975

Li Yiping the Athlete

Li Yiping was a born athlete. A discus thrower
he was full of energy, like a foal emerging from its corral
His homeroom teacher loved him and took him to bed
He wrote in his journal that he'd marry her when he grew up
It so happened that our teacher was a married woman
She was fired and sent to prison
That was major news in our little city

After graduation, he was assigned to a commune in the countryside
but there was no end to the scandals in which he was involved
One night, a girl was heard sobbing loudly in his room
People said she was good-looking and intelligent
He strutted like a rooster among the hens of our village
One after another, they recklessly threw themselves at him
To my way of thinking, he was the luckiest man alive

The next time we met was in modern-day Beijing
He'd tried his hand at the book trade
but didn't make enough to live on
He borrowed money right and left, paying little back
He said it was hard to make a living, and his life was a drag
I heard he'd founded a company but was saddled with debt
He grew a big paunch and a thick beard
I was reluctant to drink with him and share memories
He sighed and said, "I used to have beautiful women all around me"

Liu Mei

Liu Mei was demure and slender, with thick, long eyelashes
She was a creature of feelings, but mostly aloof toward me
On a night of heavy snowfall, when winter's chill bore down on us
a veteran took her to lie with him on his heated-brick bed
A guy pressed his ear to the wall and described what went on.
He heard the sound of her whimpering, as if in deep sadness
The veteran's parents stood near the bed, urging her not to feel bad
Then she and the veteran were seen going out as a couple
which irritated the commune secretary and the other males
Later, she began to distance herself from that veteran
and eventually moved in with one of the male school dropouts
As time passed, no one brought the matter up anymore
and no one bothered to cast sidelong glances at her
One evening sometime in 1977
she cooked a meal of dumplings to send me off
We ate lots of dumplings and talked late into the night
The lamp at the head of the bed flickered the whole time

Looking back, I faintly recall her haggard and anxious look
and the teardrops that flecked her long eyelashes

After twenty years or so
I went back to our small city and met with her
A few people remembered her night of sadness
They knew she'd fallen into promiscuity while a factory worker
They said that when the foreman's wife
caught her and the foreman in bed
she scratched Liu Mei's breasts and blackened her left eye

She cooked me a meal of dumplings in the singles dorm
She was emotional; her body worn down by the years
She said that life was getting harder for her
She missed the warmth and safety of home
Though she was not prejudiced against her days in the brigade,

she did feel revulsion about the nights she'd endured
especially in winter when she had no heated bed

"You're right," I said. "I also disliked those nights in the brigade
Even now, I want to keep warm on a heated-brick bed"

A Bayonet in the Night

Most people know that the life of sent-down youth was simple
We did farm work, earned points, tried to fit in with the farmers
On long nights, we drank and gambled,
and discussed the attributes of various women.
Our hubris surpassed that of the Merry Men of Liangshan
        Marshland
One night I bet them I could walk alone through the graveyard
        by the river
Taking a military bayonet in hand, I charged off into the darkness
The Yellow River at night was creepy and foreboding
Moonlight touched the water in flecks like the eyes of ghosts
A fox was so busy hunting rats he lost the urge to mount his mate
Beneath my footsteps came the subliminal sounds of wailing
A black cat hunting mice was crouching on a tree branch
On all sides fireflies blinked then hid in darkness
Chilly wind sobered me up, my heart raced crazily
Right then my ears caught an unknown moaning sound
In the pitch dark, I stumbled into a graveyard pond

Later, I went home, carrying a skull. It still had a patch of hair
Seeing it on the bed, the boys turned pale and the girls squealed

The next day I went back to the graveyard to find my bayonet
which was a key item supplied to junior cadres in the militia
It lay in the underwater stillness, its shape distinctly visible
A heap of white bones beside it sent a shiver through me
I thought the owner of those bones would want it for protection
so I'd tell the sergeant it was carried off by that black cat

Thirty years later, I returned to that spot on the riverbank
The place had turned into a bleak, featureless alkaline marsh
but a dry willow stood there, half in sun and half in gloom
I knew it was my youth that kept the bayonet company

Lil' Sis Duan

Sister of a sent-down school dropout, she was a nice sweet child
She never went past primary school, but a braid grew to her waist
She was shy and would not meet my gaze
I enjoyed seeing her when I got together with her brother
Once I brought an old-style box camera back from the city
She had no choice but to stand in front of my lens
I could finally squint my eye and look at her beautiful face
I told her this was a handy camera, but it took time to focus
She was at the point of tears when I finally snapped the shutter
In black and white, her fretful look made her even more loveable

Later, she let me ride on the back seat of her bike
While weeding fields, she let me wipe sweat with her scarf
The rising sap of youth made me sleepless at night
My fantasy was to take her away, to start a home together
I felt that the wheat was long in ear and ready for harvest
It was time for reaping the ripe sorghum and filling the granary

On the day before I left the village, I brushed past her breast
Her brother was riding up ahead but he never turned his head
A sudden move made the bike wobble but she kept us balanced
I thought she was shedding tears because she wiped her face
        with her sleeve
I thought I'd come back and carry away her affections

I didn't make it back to that village
And she never answered my letters
Years later, I visited the village again
She was already a mother, tender and capable
She still kept her head lowered, still tended to blush
She said she didn't work in the fields, just did the cooking
because her husband earned money as a migrant worker
She said she'd never received any of my letters

She said it eased her mind to see how well I was doing

That's right, and it eased my mind to see her doing well too

Miss Zhu Miaomei

Back then, I was classified as one of the "five black categories"
so I regularly underwent public denunciation in middle school
Below the stage, Zhu Xiaomei was loudest at shouting slogans
because I had once tied her braid to the back of her chair

A cadre's daughter, she disdained the children of workers
At the sight of me she pursed her lips and rolled her eyes
Dark-skinned and boisterous, she did cartwheels when she pleased
At the commune, she played girl's basketball and I played on the
     boy's team
We each played our own games, not getting in each other's way
Due to the anger I felt, she looked incomparably ugly to me
Due to disdain, she made a *hmph* sound at the sight of me

One day, having gotten overly close with a girl on her team
I shared eggs with them that I got by swapping work points
She vented her outrage by talking to herself in the cornfield
saying I was a hoodlum who had a knack for shady dealings
After that, we never looked each other in the eye again
until I was in university, riding the night train on holiday
Half awake I heard the conductor checking sleeper berths
She was checking tickets and bags, looking for fireworks
I said, "These are pickled eggs, not fireworks"
Suddenly the conductor turned away without responding
I heard her co-worker say, "Why did you stop checking?"

Years later, I attended a banquet to promote investment in our
     province
After a bout of drinking, the local leaders took me to the train
     station
The stationmaster took charge of escorting me to the sleeper car
She was being polite, but her eyes were downcast
Dark and stocky, she was more imposing than ever

There was a moment of residual fear, but I kept my composure

As my train pulled out, she bid farewell with a blast of her whistle

Prosperity Ma

Prosperity Ma came from a good background of low-to-mid-level
      farmers
In middle school he was the Red Guard who escorted me
      to denunciations
He used to press a mock rifle roughly against the back of my head
I think that must be why I often have a sore neck these days
After he was sent to a production team, our fates were reversed
I was bookkeeper for the brigade; he was just a sent-down youth

He was bull-headed and found fault with everything I said
I sent him to dig ditches or harness donkeys to a manure wagon
Perhaps due to bull-headedness, a gaping sore grew in his left ear
Day after day, he stuffed wads of paper or cotton in his ear canal
Once when he asked for sick leave, I suspended his work points
He couldn't bear to lose points, so he insisted on going to work

Finally he got over his stiff-necked attitude toward me
He sat on my bed's edge, drinking and looking miserable
He told me his parents were getting old and had many ailments
His little sister was weak; his little brother had no interest
      in studying
He needed to earn more points to buy medicine for his parents
He had only denounced me to get merit points and stay in the city

Since we were drinking, my tears started falling as well
The two of us forgot our animosity toward each other
Next day, coal miners were being recruited; I recommended him
When setting out he lost his composure and broke out sobbing

Many years later, I went home for a school dropout reunion
I didn't see him at the gathering and heard no news of him
Someone said he made foreman and ran the mine with brisk
      efficiency
Others said he was at home convalescing from silicosis

After getting drunk, I gazed out through the barroom window
I felt long-buried regrets and wished he hadn't have stayed away
    from the reunion

I saw a man with haggard features standing under a street light
He seemed stiff-necked as he stared into the bar

Women in the Fields

All the women in the fields are married; each has a bunch of kids
They are unaware of hardship and find pleasure in their work
They are capable of tackling a man and stripping off his clothes
I surmise that they've entertained thoughts of doing that to me
They tell off-color stories so depraved you've never heard them
They tell scandalous anecdotes about the sent-down youths
For instance, a pair of youths were coupling in a wheatfield
They stirred up a rat and the frightened girl ran home naked
They told about a fellow who wanted to bed his lover during the day
He told his sister to fetch corn from the roof, then removed the
        ladder
You could hear them howling and moaning inside the house
His sister's loud curses couldn't drown out their rutting noise

The women in the field taught me the facts of life
I think that was a Chinese form of sex education
Years later, I'm leading an upright, proper life
but I still miss those women in the field

Yes indeed, I miss those women in the field

Zhang Gang

Zhang Gang was a tractor driver in our production brigade
The tractor model we used back then was called "East Is Red"
Each day when the red sun rose, he'd start the engine
and rouse me to go eat the sesame buns he'd cooked
Most impressive was when we rode his tractor into the city,
just like today when someone rides in a Land Rover in Beijing
One night a cadre took a frantic shot while hunting wild dogs
The bullet pierced the tractor's rear engine housing
He sighed heavily as he repaired it, then told me why
If the bullet had hit his leg, he could rest and let it heal
Most of the eggs from his hens went into my bowl
He wouldn't waste them on themself; I looked like I needed them

On the morning I left, he came to see me off
He brought a quilt in his arms and started up "East Is Red"
He stopped at a field and threw armfuls of straw on the flatbed
He made my seat comfy, told me to take the quilt to Beijing
That day the autumn wind was not blowing on the road
but my eyes were still swimming with tears

Many years passed, and I forgot about the "East Is Red"
When I saw him next, he was riding a shuttle bus to the city
He did not drink water or eat, and he didn't have much to say
He said he was fasting, preparing for a pilgrimage to Mecca
I wanted to buy him a griddle cake with egg, which made him
        smile
He sat facing me; his posture respectfully upright
He said now that his kids were grown, he could rest easy
His abdomen felt sore on cloudy days, from driving the tractor
        over bumps
I said it was his tractor that hauled me into my new life
He said, "I don't know what you mean. I've given rides to many."

Even now I watch broadcasts about the pilgrimage to Mecca

Amid the crowd I always seem to see the shape of his body
Once I asked a newspaper reporter who wrote a financial column,
Don't you know that "East Is Red" is China's toughest, reddest brand?

The Brother of Ma Qiuyun

Ma Qiuyun was a kind-hearted teacher in our commune's charter
    school
She and I once performed as a duo on stage; she had magnetic
    appeal
She'd smile at you so sweetly, you wouldn't dare harbor ill intentions
But her older brother was an alcoholic scoundrel who had twisted
    ideas
After getting drunk, he'd unbutton the fly of his trousers
Sobbing loudly, he'd say, "Oh my pitiful cock, what can you do?
You need to prove your potency; you still haven't taken a wife
You're almost thirty and still haven't touched a woman!"
One day, the whole commune heard the news—he'd gotten married
No one could have imagined he'd find such a stunning beauty
Some called her a fox-demon from the riverside, reborn in human
    form
Some people thought up schemes to get a feel of her ethereal flesh
The male secretary of our production brigade was short and fat,
a distant cousin of Ma Qiuyun, and her brother's drinking buddy
On the wedding night, both men ended up drunk and in bed with
    the bride
Some said that the secretary was lying atop her
Ma Qiuyun's brother reported the incident to the commune
He claimed to have felt the wetness of semen on her body
Officer Duan questioned the secretary and the bride separately
To solve the case he had to dig out all sorts of details
Later Officer Duan reported that he had cracked the case
The bride described the size of the secretary's hard penis
but the secretary swore he had only fallen asleep on top of her
Ma Qiuyun's brother and his bride had devised this scheme to
    evade a debt

This earth-shaking news set the commune astir for three months
After drinks, Officer Duan would reveal the length of the bride's
    pubic hair

Afterward, Ma Qiuyun's brother still drank with the secretary
His wife cooked for them and warmed their wine
After a few drinks the secretary would confess to anyone present:
"My penis doesn't stay that hard, but it's not all that small either"

At meetings my eyes would often stray to the secretary's fly

Ma Huayin

Ma Huayin, a former student, returned to his village, a selfless soul
He did without padded shoes in winter, so the skin of his heels was
    cracked
During a mass labor project, he stitched those cracks with a sewing
    needle
Blood and mud froze together, making him stamp his feet in pain
At meals he'd fix his eyes on me; I'd give him crisp rice from the
    pan bottom
People say a man who eats half-burnt rice will have luck finding a
    wife
Hearing that, he'd nod his head and show a silly grin
Then one day he was crushed by falling rocks
I can still see his expression, as if crying yet seeming to smile
That day he was digging loads of sandy soil from a hillside
A landslide swept him downhill, tumbling down with the rocks
To those watching, it seemed he was sitting atop a wave of dirt
At times it would cover him, then he'd reappear
He was placed atop the sandy loam he'd dug to be hauled home
One of his buddies went ahead with the news, wailing the whole
    way
People sobbed as they met the tractor at the edge of the village
Ma Huayin lay stiffly, bubbles of blood coming from his mouth
His heels weren't bleeding, but I think they were still painful
He didn't look frightened, but his buddies couldn't calm down

That very day, he was buried in the dirt
I think he could finally get a good long sleep
Ever since, my heart skips at the sight of needle and thread
At the sight of rice, I feel pressure in my chest

I think all of our rice is grown in the soil he dug

Security Guard Duan

When Security Guard Duan was out walking,
his ashen face looked like a leaf adrift in a stream
The number two tractor driver in our brigade,
he was afraid of ghosts and darkness and walking alone
He swore he'd seen a ball of fire creeping toward him,
which caused him to drive the tractor into a ditch
He said our production brigade was built on old graves
He was right. I used to see foxfire flitting about at night
Shortly threafter, I was awakened late in the night
by something scratching the soles of my feet. It was only a rat
One night when the moonlight was like water
a feral cat was howling on my windowsill
I stoked up courage and drew near, gun in hand
It darted away, scrambling over things then jumping down
It jumped on the blacksmith's stove, and I nailed it with one shot
Under the moonlight, its eyes looked like little green lamps
The next day I went to check on it, but the spot was empty
There was nothing there, no sign of anything being killed

Duan said it was a ghost and warned me to watch out
because my bed was over what had been a grave
Not until my quilt was ignited by coals under my bed
did I think it was time to sleep in a different place
But Duan also said, "Don't bother,
but be sure to wash your feet before bed"

I believed I definitely needed to wash my feet before bed
but I didn't like going to the stream at night
I was afraid to be alone in the dark
Even now, in the city, I fear being alone in darkness

Li Hua

Li Hua, a young returnee, was dogged by rotten luck
While cycling downhill, his wheel-fork broke, breaking his three
     front teeth
After that, whether speaking or not, he seemed to hide a secret
From then on, finding a wife became bothersome
In August when the wheat ripened, we went to deliver our quota
     of grain
He slipped from the running board, and a falling bag ruptured his
     colon
At the local hospital, with blood and feces oozing, they stitched
     him up
After that he never straightened his waist again when walking
It put him on edge to see girls but he couldn't get over his shyness
He was a good person, but no girl wanted to marry him
During militia training, he helped me bundle sticks of dynamite
He often went to the riverside and caught fish using explosives

Later his father and grandpa used their harvest to arrange a
     marriage
We all chipped in to put on a wedding banquet for him
He wanted to build a house, but he never got approval for lumber
So he went to the river to pull out driftwood and floating branches
One day he slipped into the water and disappeared
We threw sticks of dynamite into the river, hoping to raise his body
The bundles of dynamite he made were the biggest
They caused fish and turtles to float belly-up in a daze
Old folks thought he'd offended the dragon king with his blasting
We all noticed that the fish floating up were weirdly deformed

Later, Li Hua's body was found near the riverbank
We found catfish in his belly, gnawing at his vitals

Officer Duan

Officer Duan was far from fastidious; his stained teeth
     looked like manure
He spit up phlegm and flicked strings of snot, always shouting
     and growling
He sometimes hog-tied people and left them by the side of the road
He said I could raid the melon patch with my militiamen at night
The next day he'd check out the site and crack the case
claiming that fox demons needed cold melon platters
     for a wedding banquet
because the foxes couldn't manage with stir-fried rabbit alone
One day, sure enough, they mounted a sudden attack on a fox den
and captured five little kits, lively and loveable
His wife gave them food; from then on, her sex-drive became
     voracious
He feared going home, so he spent his time patrolling the
     countryside
His police cap sat crooked on his head, his rifle hung aslant
One day the little foxes attempted to run off in all directions
With well-aimed bricks, Officer Duan wiped them out one by one
Meanwhile his wife stood watching, her mouth agape
     in astonishment
From then on, he flexed his chest and whistled with his head
     held high

One day he ordered me to go out hunting foxes
He said foxes are demons that need to be shot and buried deep
I went running along the river, a German-made Mauser in hand,
thinking that since I wasn't married, I needn't treat foxes
     as something terrible
Officer Duan kept shooting into the sky and shouting hoarsely
The foxes couldn't stand the commotion; they jumped in the river
     and fled

Sparrows at Harvest Time

Sparrows come flying above the Yellow River in fall
Like yellow waves, their flock drills into space; charges through
      the sky
Soft yellow tufts at their beak corners, they fly all over the world
They bear children and shit and piss right here in my wheatfield
Like vagabonds of the earth, they go about, natural and carefree
They flutter before my eyes and see me as a walking skeleton
While I'm beating on a gong, they do a dance atop the wheat ears
When I'm about to set off fireworks, they make themselves scarce
In my months of industrious planting, where did they go off to?
To be sure, those years had already been stolen from me
Before I'd sharpened my scythe, their beaks were already polished
I was born into a terrible era for sent-down youth
Wheat kernels are strewn about in golden drops by sparrows
My work points decrease, bead by bead, on the abacus
I shout at the sparrows, "Get outta here"
To hell with it, this broken-down sparrow world

Cats Buried Alive

Today I got myself a new burlap bag
I think it'll probably hold twenty dead cats
Grandma Liu tearfully hands her Hua-hua to me
It makes no peep inside the bag, as if it died twice already
I am the Grim Reaper of cats, haunting the alleyways
I am the killer of living souls, I am a destroyer of worlds
An old cat in a corner obediently lets itself be captured
The miasma of death makes it give up all resistance
Old cats await my burlap bag beneath the sunflowers
Last night my government ordered their liquidation
because they ate up field rats too greedily
and field rats are the carriers of black death
I'm a school dropout; their fate is not mine to decide
I can only kill or capture them to earn work points
At dusk I bury the burlap bag deep underground
On top of them, the earth seems to quiver

A Villager Hit by an Ice Chunk

That was a winter of nose-nipping cold
but we had to lay explosive charges for blasting ice
because we had to clear a long irrigation ditch
and make preparations for next year's harvest
While burying the charges, I had an urge to urinate
I think that was an omen of a horrific incident
As my piss froze into a yellow spot on the earth's skin
I heard a charge go off behind me; it was half-a-minute early
A human-shape without an arm was thrown into the air
I think that was Bigtooth Li, grimacing down at me
Auntie Liu in her red headscarf was hit by a chunk of ice
She went rolling on the ground like a log
The sound of the blast seemed to last for a century
followed by a century of terrifying silence
I laid down in silence, imagining that I, too, was dead
Good grief! We laid those charges, and villagers died in the blast

Militia Vow-Taking Ceremony

The commune hosted a vow-taking ceremony for the militia
Due to the Lin Biao issue, we swore our fidelity to Chairman Mao
The villagers said I looked like a German foreigner
with my 50 calibre assault rifle at my chest, wiry and on-edge
We paraded on the deserted dirt road through the village
our steps in unison, stirring dust that hung in the air
Big roosters and old hens ran away at the sound
In loud voices, we sang songs of the revolutionary proletariat
The brown ox didn't know how to yield the right of way
It stuck out its horns as if glowering at the people's militia
We solemnly marched around it
Not bothering to notice, it squeezed out a heap of manure
on barren ground. We shouted slogans and sang revolutionary
       songs
The sparrows flew off, the frogs jumped into the water
Later, we fell out of step, and on a day I can't clearly recall
we proclaimed ourselves disbanded

About "Ghosts Carrying a Sedan Chair"

As bookkeeper for the production brigade, I watched over
    the brigade office
When night fell I wedged the door shut with my bayonet
Because the office was built on an old, untended graveyard
I couldn't fall asleep without running my hands over a Mauser
    repeater
Some people say they saw foxfire floating in front and back
    of the house
And I could almost hear low sobs from the moon half-hidden
    by clouds
The villagers called this phenomenon "Ghosts Carrying a Sedan
    Chair"
Those souls don't like having their territory infringed upon
    by living people
One night a half-human, half-cat thing made crying-laughing
    noises
I wrapped myself in a blanket which was damp with cold sweat
That thing bumped against the window, calling to me in a low
    voice
It finally provoked me into cocking my gun, going out to fight for
    my life
I ran through the graveyard, chasing a wisp of shadow
I raised my arms and fired off a clip of bullets
At daybreak I found a pitiful cat, lying dead beside some bones
It had been hit by several bullets; it's wide eyes were glaring

Hopeless Journey Home

I'd have to say, that was a hopeless rainy spell
That day could be called a hopeless journeying home
I was riding my bike through mud back to the village
Actually, I was the one who seemed like a hopeless loser
I carried my bike for a stretch, my tears falling in the rain
In the scrublands, I looked like a hairless stray dog
sloshing in the mud, past the point of being worn and tired
I thought that jumping in the river might be some kind of release
No sound of rain or river; no sound on the barren ground
I kept going alone, mind and body both cold
I thought of the dry warmth of my bed
imagining a time when my luck might finally change
Then I'd be walking down a clean street, umbrella in hand
Lamplight looks blurry but inviting in the rain
Imagining the comfort, I slipped and fell in the wasteland
In the gloom, I hopelessly closed my eyes

Accountant Huang

I am Accountant Huang, and I have plenty of power
The official seal and abacus are in my keeping
For weddings and funerals villagers need letters from me
Quotas for bicycles and lumber are under my control
My work points are highest, so I can spend lavishly
So I often drink yam liquor, which costs 1.18 yuan
Villagers gain face if I appear at their wedding banquets
Cross-legged on my bed, I play both sides of "finger guessing"
In fact, I often pour shots of liquor into my covered teacup
The villagers pretend they don't notice
I gladly put in half a yuan when sharing the cost of a bottle
Being a former student, I don't take part in wedding-night parties
but someone tells me later about listening at the bedroom door
As Accountant Huang, I must maintain an impressive demeanor
For instance, in the fields, I squat on my haunches while speaking
and I always carry a fountain pen in my shirt pocket
for keeping accounts and recording Accountant Huang's days

The Bugler

The bugler never had a chance to join the Army, but he sure could
        play the trumpet
Because of his pitted face, he always walked with his head down
He mainly played "Reveille," "Fatigue Call," and "Call to Quarters"
Of course, of all the calls he played, we thought "Recall" was best
His brass bugle was shiny as red satin
At sunset and sunrise, he always played facing the sun
He didn't have to dig ditches, which made everyone jealous
Some said his pocked face would make it hard to find a wife
When he'd had the pox, his grandma couldn't find a pigeon to heal
        him
He knew by that omen that fate had dire times in store for him
While talking, he held his bugle tight, not knowing what to do
        with his hands
Later, people no longer ridiculed him behind his back
He was just a child who became a bugler
He held his head high while bugling, but lowered it while walking
His bugle calls urged worn-down troops to go into the world
to dig dirt and carry mud from dawn until the sun's last rays

White Rabbit Creamy Candy

Liu Mei was a girls' school dropout; her father went on assignment
    to Beijing
I gave her five yuan so he could buy me White Rabbit Creamy Candy
She liked me, so she chipped in another five yuan
and her father brought back a large box of it
I had wished for this since childhood
My mother had been too poor to grant my wish
After she was laid in her grave and I became Accountant Huang
I wanted that candy, to make up for her regret
The candy was made in Shanghai, which I imagined as heaven
and it came through Beijing, which in my mind was sacred ground
When I could finally eat my fill of it, I felt sorrow in my heart
I'd become, at last, a fortunate son among the Chinese people,
an accountant for a production brigade, an earner of work points
I ate candy all day, until the sweetness felt unpleasant on my teeth
This is a memory of candy's revenge and of how we lived
After that, milk candy was most repulsive thing I could think of

A Snowy New Year's Night

One snowy New Year's night, I really had nowhere to go
I lay still on my bed, feeling feverish and spouting nonsense
On the third day, a villager barged in and took me away
He trudged through the snow, pulling a beat-up old handcart,
At his house I broke out crying again and again
I spoke of things neither my listeners nor I understood
The villagers said I must have been possessed by an *yíbulísí*
They chanted some kind of verse for me, until they got red-eyed
After my fever broke, I stared vapidly at the ceiling for seven days
The oldsters secretly commented: "The poor child is turning mute"
When I ate my first mouthful of spaetzle, I smiled a bit
then shed two teardrops into my bowl
My quilt was warm, but my body odor was foul
I think that my organs were probably decomposing
Since then I've been fond of flowery patterns on quilts and clothes
On snowy nights, I feel a chill in my heart

A Red Flag Brand Bicycle

My "Red Flag" bike was an extra-strong model
When I carried it through mud it felt really heavy
In my sent-down days it was the symbol of my identity
With a flick of the ringer, it made a loud zingy sound
It could carry two school dropouts, one up front and one behind
Of course, the girls always sat up front as I pedaled
On the way to work, its firm tires crushed lots of toads
It was still dark at dawn, and no light gleamed on the dew
Riding that bike, I felt that I could ride to the world's end
Streaking over the wasteland, I felt like a Chinese Don Quixote
This was my private property, so it carried the years of my life
I used it to carry wheat and eggs and anti-tank mines
When the wheel fork broke, I welded it back together
but from then on, it was like an old man with a handicap
The whole frame made constant creaking noises
which put me in an irritable, uneasy frame of mind
Seeing its rust spots, I surmised they were bad omens
I pressed the ringer, but I did not hear a peep

A Haystack by the Village Entrance

On summer nights I'd often sleep on a haystack at village edge
Little sparrows squabbled in their nests near where I lay
Their wild movements gave pause to the blue cat that hunted them
I surmised that the cat was a messenger for some kind of ghoul
A parade of field rats would slink out from the haystack
to seize little frogs and eat them as a delicacy
Courting couples hurried to the base of the haystack
in moments of passion, thumped their legs like rabbits
then left just as fast
Residual cooking smoke drifted sideways over the haystack
from the Ma house, where they kneaded cornmeal into spaetzle
I could strip naked due to mugginess and look up at the stars
Such vastness made me think I'd die upon entering dreamland
As crickets jumped on my forehead, I felt my own cold tears
I missed living with my mother; I missed being in love
After summer nights, the haystack became horse fodder
Gripping a straw cutter, I chopped the dry, golden stems to bits

Sneaky Adulterer

A sneaky adulterer might be someone with consummate skill
He goes about the village at night; no trace of him is seen
He actually strips naked and leaves his clothes near the wall
then climbs through a window and into a woman's bed
Someone roused by all the noise might ask the woman what it was
She'd say a cat had been howling at her window, now it was gone
Moonlight would often be shining brightly on the garden bed
Sounds of crickets and frogs might still be heard
Then one day at dawn, his little pile of clothing is gone
The adulterer paces along the wall, not knowing how to get home
He suspects a cat has taken them to make a nest for her new litter
so he listens for sounds of that cat along the base of every wall
The household dogs are alarmed, which leads to frenzied barking
The man hops and spins about to protect his buttocks
People in other rooms get up to chase the cat and beat the dogs
He hides himself amid clumps of grass and mimics a cat's meow
Someone shouts, "There's a changeling cat, with no hair!"
Next evening, all the villagers are busy chasing cats

Fishing for Carp

I suppose you could call carp the genie of the Yellow River
Whiskers extended, it breaks through the water's surface
With its long tubular torso, it likes to stir up waves
It gobbles up frogs and field rats that venture into the river
but its favorite gourmet treat is a drowned human being
While rooting in bottom mud it might even dig up an eyeball
Even when we cook a dish of carp marinated in soy sauce
it glares, mouth puckered, as if staring right through us
But I know enough to catch a rat and use it to bait a hook
Until it bursts into view and rides the roiled waves
it thrashes and splashes about like a naked man having a fit
a man who is totally shameless and too agitated to care
It almost scares me into dropping the fishing rod
By then it seems like the henchman of an ancient river demon
to the point that I feel residual fear while eating its flesh
I imagine how much I'll suffer if it gets a chance to eat me
I'm a sent-down youth who has no wish to gobble everything up
I only fish for carp because I'm starving

Tax Collector Chen

Tax Collector Chen has a motorcycle
His main job is to ride it everywhere collecting taxes
Wherever people are butchering oxen or sheep, he'll appear
Five yuan per ox, three per sheep
His demands are blind to friendship
His strong point is that even a pretty lady's flirting will do no good
Just think how hard it is these days to find a good tax collector
Actually, there is something even Collector Chen cannot resist:
to ride across the river and go hunting in the East Mountains
He gets excited seeing testicles on a fleeing yellow antelope
and likes the goatish smells and male organs coming into sight
While giving chase he's more worked up than the male antelope
to the point that he often forgets to pull the trigger
and the antelopes run off in couples across the desert
He is always alone, madly chasing one couple after another
One day, Collector Chen ran out of gas out there in the desert
He walked for three days and nights, like an antelope that lost its herd
He was punished for the loss of his motorcycle
After that he hardly spoke, and his body gave off a goatish smell

Foul-Smelling Buns

Water along the river gets too high, leaving patches of alkaline soil
Villagers hadn't been able to grow vegetables for many years
so they crushed steamed buns and fermented them into a sauce
This condiment flavored my diet in my school-dropout days
After work I'd sit under the eaves, watching a granny make
       steamed buns
then put them in a crock and bury them underground
I knew that ten days later, they could be used as a sauce
In those bitter days, you had to stomach bitter-tasting things
I imagined those buns splitting open and spoiling inside the crock
and wondered if they'd smell as foul in the future as they did now
The granny said, "Brother, if you like eating it, take all you want"
I saw the small child beside her shedding tears over it
I'd become a person who scraped food from the dirt
What we got from dirt was put into the dirt to alter the flavor
I smeared the fermented paste over my rice and ate every grain
Ever since then, memories of my youth give off a moldy odor

The Transformer Thief

A person was slumped dead over a transformer
fifteen meters above the ground and flecked with frost
Public security said he was a thief who'd tried to steal it
A girl in the village shouted, "How could that be my brother?"
Beside her was her sister-in-law, who'd just married into the family
The sister-in-law just stared wide-eyed, without saying a thing
Stealing such a thing was sabotage, a counter-revolutionary act
There were grounds for death, so no one dared make a fuss
I never saw that girl again,
but someone saw her acting crazy in the city
Each morning, rays would shine on that transformer
Luckily, nobody else has ended up hanging there
One day the high-voltage line snapped in a fierce wind
The transformer caught on fire and turned into scrap metal
so people abandoned it in the field
not far from where that thief lies

Singing "Lan Hua-hua"

A cloudy day at dusk, the Yellow River was turbid and slow
It flowed out of one cloud bank and into another
Ma Yucheng tensed his throat to hit the notes of "Orchid Flower"
I wanted to cry, but also to jump into the river's current
One hand gripping his ragged coat, he faced the clouds and sang
He said a girl named "Orchid Flower" lived on the other bank
Back then you would get in no end of trouble for singing that song
"Lan Hua-hua" had been classed as an obscene, erotic song
but we were really sick of hoeing in the fields all day long
He sang and I listened without making any fuss
He was illiterate, but tears sparkled on his lashes as he sang
He held the long notes as if floating over the water
The wide river stretched a great distance, with no boat in sight
I could imagine Orchid Flower's beauty before my eyes
Standing at water's edge, I stared intently at the other bank
Across the river a string of camels was striding into the distance
After that day, a school-dropout pined for Orchid Flower

A Swineherd

Being of Chinese ethnicity, I am required to go purchase pigs
but herding pigs is really hard; their pen is fifteen klicks away
Like wild geese at the river's edge, they disregard instructions
and wallow and root with an air of pampered privilege
When they scatter I chase them back and forth like a sheep dog
When they plant their feet in water, I bellow like a crocodile
With their little eyes, they observe my every movement
With my wasp-like eyes, I gather them into my field of vision
I point to the sun and shout that wolves will eat them after dark
With switching tails, they reply that life or death is up to Heaven
My shoe falls off in mud; the chill pierces my foot to the quick
Water soaks my coat and trousers; the wind freezes my heart
As a school dropout I must herd swine; where's the sense in that?
Having left the city, I have no home; will there be a tomorrow?
The pigs dawdle in disorder, with disdain for my private concerns
When I close the pigpen, I stare woodenly at the latch
The pigs are happy with the mud puddle in their new home
Where will my new home be: in a coal mine or in Yinchuan City?

Eating a Camel's Foot

Before its last breath, an imam drained the dying camel's blood
My share was the camel's foot, meaty and tough
After ten hours of stewing in a basin, it gave off a hearty smell
Dogs and cats came running from the fields
In height of summer, oleaster by the ditches gave off a heady scent
I quietly chewed on the foot, imagining the expression of a camel
Since I was a school-dropout, dogs and cats did not run off with it
Since I was an accountant, villagers refrained from dropping by
That was a revolutionary era; I had to stuff myself full
Those were days of hardship; a camel wouldn't die every day
My hands, calloused by shovels, could tear apart camel meat
My stomach, fed on sorghum and corn, was getting a warm feeling
That was a whole camel's foot, king-sized and delicious
That was an era that won't let itself be forgotten
Three days later, I was still eating that camel's foot
After that the villagers said I looked like a camel when I walked

A Record of Killing Dogs

The plague was spreading so we had to kill all dogs and cats
As I hefted my rifle, my heart filled with murderous intent
Haunting the fields and village lanes, I was the century's hit man
From two hundred meters my bullet hit a fleeing black dog
      in the heart
A boy came leading his dog and cried watching me pull the trigger
An old lady said, "No problem, you're educated and won't be
      held accountable"
A family of three dogs took an afternoon nap on the threshing
      ground
I raised my gun and shot the parents while the pup whimpered
      in a dream
Dogs ran to tell their kind: "One of the educated youths is a murderer"
They hid themselves in cornfields; they ran along the riverbank
I possessed uncountable bullets and unlimited power as a killer
and I had untold frustrations and vexations over my
      unknown future
My semiautomatic was beat-up, but bullets didn't jam
Bodies of my victims decayed and gave off foul odors in the sun
Next year trees would grow greener because of this
In the coming year there'd be deathly silence in fields and village
After killing the 312th dog, I washed my hands
At bedtime, I wedged the door shut with a bayonet

A Record of Hunting Wild Geese

The geese had returned and were dabbling for food near the river
I snuck close to them like a wolf, crawling on my knees
In one hand was a .38 carbine with long, shiny bayonet
It killed Chinese during the War, and now it would shoot geese
Fresh from their spring migration, those honking birds were on edge
One goose stood guard on a high place, not eating or drinking
I rubbed spit on a brass cartridge, chambered it, and took aim
At this hundred-meter distance, I could kill anything in the world
The geese stayed close to one another, sunning their tired wings
They ate jumping grasshoppers and seeds from our spring planting
Goose feathers floated on the sluggish Yellow River current
I slowly squeezed the trigger, hoping I'd have good luck
A pan full of goose flesh would make my days much less dreary
Silenced by the gunshot, the geese leaned their heads together
The guard goose's wings unfolded, its neck stretched in the mud
As I lifted my prey, the heavens turned dark
The flock of geese skimmed overhead more than once
It was spring, the guard goose was not very heavy
Enough for a quick stir-fry with two drams of yam liquor
And yet, every time I drank after that, I'd get drunk
The flock of geese did not return to that riverbank

A Record of Losing a Cat

I am an educated youth, and I have a leopard cat
It keeps me company with carefree antics through any weather
At dawn I harness a cart and haul manure to work the fields
It stretches its four limbs and goes on dozing on my bed
By day I use an abacus, keep accounts, fill out forms for the brigade
The cat brings mice that it caught in the storeroom next door
I have never seen it chomping on mice or baring its teeth
The mice always play dead then slink away to freedom
The cat toys with them, as if with figures made of its favorite treat
so it doesn't mind me blowing my nose or rattling the abacus beads
In summer it climbed the eaves after baby sparrows, but instead
          found a snake
It fell yowling to the ground, then disappeared for three days
When nestlings fell on the ground, it would jump around in circles
which brought a lot of swallows, twittering and crying
Mornings, I freshened up at a stream while it viewed itself
          in the water
It refused to let me wipe its paws or wash its nose with cold water
At nighttime, while I read Marx or wrote love letters under a lamp
its eyes were half-closed, but it wouldn't let itself fall asleep
One day while sunning itself on a sill, it was carried off
Only then did I realize that I had never given it a name

Reading Marx and Lenin

The good thing about an earthen bed is that you can pile on books
At night, when the bed is warmed, one's ardor is sure to intensify
Das Kapital told me the why of revolution, but *Anti-Dühring* puzzled me
Back then we pretended to understand everything thoroughly
In the fields, I expounded to girls about Chernyshevsky's *What Is to
    Be Done*
I could see the sad looks behind their long, thick eyelashes
On winter walls I painted "Our Socialist Motherland Is Advancing
    Victoriously"
I wrapped my jacket around the paint bucket, but my lips were
    frozen blue
A night procession against Lin Biao was held near the river,
    with real guns
Under bright stars our loud slogans scared the foxes from their dens
Our hearts burned with indignation, so we opened fire on them
Having used up our bullets, we went home and slept soundly
Thenceforth while singing "The Troika" in bed, I was always
    off pitch
I never wore new clothes; my pants were held up by straw rope
I made sure to sew at least seven patches on my clothes
I had to distinguish "the weapon of criticism" from "criticism of
    weapons"
I couldn't let sheep belonging to bad guys start eating socialist grass
By lamplight I wept over *The Gadfly* and *Notes from the Gallows*
I used to cradle my .50 calibre rifle and polish it to a bright sheen
In the vastness of heaven and earth, great things would be done
We would never, ever become the sprouts of capitalism

Afterward

"Afterward" implies the passing of days and years
but I still feel like a school dropout, still counting work points
By arithmetical calculations I got my name on the Forbes List
In my persona as Accountant Huang, I figure out my finances
Some days I think, "This may a good time to go back
in my guise as a city dweller, showing my rich man's face"
The first time I went, one person directed cold words at me
"What a hypocrite! Weren't you going to put down lifelong roots?"
I thought, "To hell with you. What kind of talk is that?
This is your village. What gives you the right to say I should stay?"
Someone else told me he was doing fairly well in life
He had cows and sheep; he was filling in at the middle school
I said, "We're all doing pretty well; we're living in a good era".
The second time I went, someone wanted me to open my wallet
because his ailments were getting worse, with no one to help
That brought tears to my eyes, and I paid for his hospital stay
I also helped him with gifts of clothing for his children
Someone else said his house was ready to fall apart
He needed to buy land and bricks, to find a wife for his son
The third time I built a kindergarten for the village children
It was spacious and built to be safe in a magnitude 8 earthquake
Those running, jumping kids had no idea who I was
Their teacher said I was a school dropout who appeared on TV
The fourth time, I paced up and down the main street of the town
I wanted to let tears fall, to cry out that those years were bullshit
In fact, I never really became a tiller of the soil
Being adrift is a deep-seated part of my emotional life

Notes on the Poems

Page 17: A catty is approximately 500 grams, or just over 1 pound.

1.18 Yuan is approximately 17 cents U.S.

Page 19: Lin Daojing was the female protagonist in *Song of Youth* by Yang Mo (Qingchun zhi ge, 1958), a novel about the idealistic youths who participated in underground work for the Communist Party before WWII.

The Gadfly (1897) by the Irish-born author Ethel Voynich is a novel about the Italian revolution. It is a tale of faith, disillusionment, revolution, romance, and heroism.

Page 21: The Helan Mountains are an isolated desert mountain range forming the border of Inner Mongolia's Alxa League and Ningxia.

The Qingming Festival, known as Tomb-Sweeping Day in English, is a traditional Chinese celebration of spring. It falls in early April on the 15th day after the Spring Equinox. Chinese families visit the tombs of their ancestors to clean the gravesites and make ritual offerings to their ancestors. The holiday recognizes the traditional reverence of one's ancestors in Chinese culture.

Page 25: Merry Men of Liangshan Marsh - Based upon the historical bandit Song Jiang and his companions, this Chinese equivalent of the English classic Robin Hood and His Merry Men is an epic tale of rebellion against tyranny and has been thrilling and inspiring readers for hundreds of years.

Page 28: The word *cadre* most broadly refers to a full-time, professional revolutionary dedicated to the goals of a communist party, who works at the discretion of its leadership.

The "Five Black Categories" were defined during the Chinese Cultural Revolution (1966–1976) by Mao Zedong, who ordained that people in these groups should be considered enemies of the Revolution. The groups were: landlords, rich farmers, counter-revolutionaries, bad influencers, and right-wingers. Conversely, Mao categorized groups of people, such as members of the Chinese Communist Party, poor farmers and low class workers, as Five Red Categories. This new Red/Black class distinction was used to create a status society. People in the Five Black Categories were separated out for struggle sessions, humiliation, re-education, beating, and persecution. Mao believed that victimizing these people was necessary to initiate the changes in Chinese culture that he desired.

Page 30: Silicosis is a lung disease caused by breathing in tiny bits of silica found in various rocks. It mainly affects miners.

Page 33: "The East Is Red" tractor was marketed under the brand Dongfanghong, now YTO Global. The company was founded in 1955 and became the largest manufacturer of tractors in China. "East is Red" was also a Communistt Party revolutionary song that was the de facto national anthem of the People's Republic of China during the Cultural Revolution.

Page 38: Foxfire is the bioluminescence created by some species of fungi present in decaying wood.

Page 44: The Lin Bao incident - On the night of September 12-13, 1971, Lin Biao, Mao Zedong's officially recognized closest comrade-in-arms and chosen successor, was killed in a mysterious plane crash in Mongolia. The Chinese government did not issue an announcement of Lin's death, and it became generally known only in the summer of 1972, when the official explanation stated that Lin had masterminded plans for a coup d'état and the assassination of Mao, and died fleeing to the Soviet Union after both plans had failed. But no convincing proof was offered to substantiate these claims, and the Lin Biao incident has remained an unsolved mystery.

Page 47: "finger guessing" - Both players extend any number of fingers on one or both hands, revealing their hands at the same time. Just before the reveal, one player must shout out a number between two and twenty. If the total number of fingers held up is equal to the sum guessed, that player is safe. If not, he or she must drink.

Page 48: In traditional Chinese medicine, pigeon meat is used as a medicinal ingredient for ailments, including pox.

Page 49: White Rabbit Creamy Candy is a brand of milk candy manufactured by Shanghai Guan Sheng Yuan Food, Ltd., in China. It is an iconic cultural brand and has been in production since 1943.

Page 50: Yibulisi is a word used by members of the Hui Minority, meaning "demon."

Page 52: The "Russian Blue Cat" or "Archangel Blue" is a cat breed with colors that vary from a light, shimmering silver to a darker, slate gray.

Page 56: A klick is a military term meaning kilometer.

Page 64: *Anti-Dühring* (1878) by Frederick Engels was a popular work which attempted to present an encyclopedic survey of philosophical, scientific and historical problems.

Nikolay Chernyshevsky (1828–1889) was a Russian journalist and socialist philosopher, often identified as a utopian socialist and a theoretician of Russian nihilism. His novel *What Is to Be Done* was published in 1863.

"The weapon of criticism cannot, of course, replace criticism of the weapon, material force must be overthrown by material force; but theory also becomes a material force as soon as it has gripped the masses." —Karl Marx.

Notes from the Gallows (1949), by an anti-Nazi partisan named Julius Fuchik, is the memoir of his imprisonment by the Gestapo in Prague during World War II.

The Poet

Luo Ying is the pen name of Huang Nubo, who holds a Ph.D. in Literature from Peking University. He authored the novel *Conch of Mount Everest* and the scholarly monograph, *Nothingness and Blossoming: Reconstructing Modernity in Contemporary Chinese Poetry* (Peking University Press). He has published eleven poetry collections including *7+2 :A Mountain Climber's Journal* (White Pine Press) and *Memories of the Cultural Revolution* (Oklahoma University Press), both published in English translation in the United States. His work has also been translated into French, German, Japanese, Korean, Turkish, Mongolian, Spanish and Icelandic.

He is an intrepid mountaineer and a key member of the Explorers Club in New York City. He has successfully climbed the highest peaks on all seven continents, including three ascents of Mount Everest, and reached the North and South Poles on foot. A successful Chinese real estate developer and entrepreneur, he founded and remains chairman of Beijing Zhongkun Investment Group. He has also founded the Zhongkun Group Poetry Development Fund, the Sino-Japanese Poetry Fund, and the Sino-Icelandic Poetry Fund. He serves as vice-president of the China Poetry Association and standing deputy-dean of the China Poetry Institute at Peking University, where he started the first Poet-in-Residence program.

Luo Ying has initiated many international poetry festivals and has established exchanges among Chinese and South American poets. He also established the Zhongkun International Poetry Prize, sponsored by the China Poetry Institute at Peking University.

Currently engaged in a ten-year plan to visit all the world's cultural heritage sites, Luo Ying strives to protect the environment and its creatures. He is a board member of WildAid International and chairman of WildAid China.

Luo Ying's website is www.luoying.me.

The Translator

Denis Mair is a translator and poet, and the author of *Man Cut in Wood*. He holds an M.A. in Chinese from Ohio State University. For many years he was a research fellow at the Hanching Academy, an institute of Chinese culture and comparative religion at Sun Moon Lake, Taiwan. He is currently a translation consultant for the Zhong-kun Cultural Fund in Beijing and translator for Jidi Majia. Among his translations are Yang Ke's *Two Halves of the World Apple*, Luo Ying's *Memories of the Cultural Revolution, 7+2 A Mountain Climber's Journal* (White Pine Press, 2020) and *Water Sprite* (White Pine Press, 2024), as well as the anthology *Poetry and Art of Yan Li*.